The Note She Left

SUSAN HAHN

The Note She Left

POEMS

NORTHWESTERN UNIVERSITY PRESS

EVANSTON, ILLINOIS

Northwestern University Press
www.nupress.northwestern.edu

Copyright © 2008 by Susan Hahn. Published 2008 by Northwestern
University Press. All rights reserved.

Printed in the United States of America

10 9 8 7 6 5 4 3 2 1

Library of Congress Cataloging-in-Publication Data

Hahn, Susan.
    The note she left : poems / Susan Hahn.
      p. cm.
    ISBN-13: 978-0-8101-2486-8 (cloth : alk. paper)
    ISBN-10: 0-8101-2486-6 (cloth : alk. paper)
    ISBN-13: 978-0-8101-2487-5 (pbk. : alk. paper)
    ISBN-10: 0-8101-2487-4 (pbk. : alk. paper)
    I. Title.
  PS3558.A3238N68 2008
  811.54—dc22

2007042941

∞ The paper used in this publication meets the minimum requirements
of the American National Standard for Information Sciences—Permanence
of Paper for Printed Library Materials, ANSI Z39.48-1992.

For Fred and Rick

*My imagination is a monastery
and I am its monk.*

—KEATS

WIDDERSHINS

AFTERWOR(L)D

ACKNOWLEDGMENTS

Grateful acknowledgment is made to the generous editors of the following publications in which these poems, or versions of them, first appeared:

The Atlantic Monthly: "Clean"

Boulevard: "Widdershins"

The Kenyon Review: "The Bells," "Knowledge" (which appeared in the short story "The Lovers")

New England Review: "The Crosses"

This book was conceived and completed with the assistance of a grant from the John Simon Guggenheim Memorial Foundation. I hope that my writings during the time of their most generous gift repay them in some small measure.

The Note She Left

The Bells

I

All night I heard the clack
of deer hooves tied to a stick
and someone beating stretched skin
over a hollow, and hoped
the sounds would appease the gods,
allow me to rise.
All night no days

would arrive. Only the fouled white
of a pig's tooth used as a clapper
inside a hard cup of clay
brought a decayed sense of light.
As the fever ran high, then higher,

an elephant heaved, her neck clamped
with a bell made of wood, her thud
a warning to curl farther away.
Soon sounds made with gold,
silver, stone and all that floods
out of the ground drowned
my head, my mind—an infant's
fistful of pebbles locked in a rattle.

II

The bell inside the tomb is silent.
It lies still as the mummy.
It does not scare away the furies

or stop the saints from their unending
prayers—warnings about sin and hell.
About sin and hell—

the dancing girl sews silver bells into
the hem of her skirt. Each move she makes
dazzles. The ringing inside

the catacombs of my ears
is a purgatory that can take me
higher or lower. The saints and furies

watch and wait, while I think
about the bell inside
the tomb and the mummy so still.

III

They turned the bell upside
down. My skin an over-
heated chamber.
Streams of vapor seeped
from my crown.
The bell cup caught
all toxic thoughts.
Then, they carried it
to a bog and buried it,
while I lay cool on calm
sheets in the silent
evening hour and gone
was the screaming fate,

left, just a small eternal sound—
silver traveling through waste.

IV

My voice—no maiden peal
of perfection—out of tune
with low hollow notes, I bathe
my throat with salt water
to make it more demon proof.
Yet foul words still bellow

out past the sign of the cross
made on my neck—my right thumb
dipped in oil leaves me
with just a grease feel.
While up the street my neighbor
stands washed, baptized, and blessed.
5 Paternosters, 5 Aves

drive all deceits of Satan away,
all dangers of whirlwind, thunder,
lightning. The fury darts
of the Devil flip backward
into my yard. She watches

from across the alley, her voice so high
with a wave of *Hi.* She who hears
only chime and ring, her soul
anchored so deep inside. She knows
no toll. My fists

beat on an old kettle
she does not possess,
to frighten away the spirits,
who find me
a tired joke, a cliché.

They step out, all
cool and slouch,
to take a smoke.

V

The shadows are longer
on my side of the world.

On yours they must be shorter
because of the earth's balance—curve.

My matter heavier.

Yours a feather?

All light trapped larger in the small
room that I question.

Does it matter?

This unraveling of atoms
existing forever, waiting to be
again. My mind's gone dark
and wild and pathless.

Yours bright and tame and secure?

I pray for direction—a sweet gate bell.

Like yours.

To ring me out of here,
but when notes come they're rung
backward as in alarm.

Do you know of harm?

I blanch in my corner
from any vibration that could allow
the delicate, poised snow to be shaken
to avalanche.

I imagine your blank face,
your sure hand
as you place picked garden
flowers in a cut-glass vase.

VI

Chime bell, triangle, harp—
little orchestra of the heart.
The vibrations beat long after
trapped energy is hit.
Even though I yell *Stop,*
they will not.

Tick tock. I am lost

in my room, shades drawn,
the town's crier.
Skeleton death knocks the inside
of my skull with a bone.

Of course, it won't stop.

I am the clock. The bell. The *belle*
so sensitive to touch—
a finger pressed against my surface
and I crack. With set mouth
uppermost about to balance
I am swung to the opposite.

*Didn't you know bells
are always feminine?*

VII

So in tune with itself—
most harmless noise
in the harm-filled world—little bell
tangled in my brain
with jangled notions
and explosions of outside bombs—

clock chimes, too heavy with measures
of forethought even for the carillonneur—forefinger and thumb
that go beyond fist and blow, to gun.

It's called Reality, they answered
to my every question.

A sledgehammer slamming sound
into the mud, the music arrives alone
from the belfry moon in its distant tower,
its light holding still the sea,
only the sky angelic trills and runs.

I could not stop looking up.

While beneath, all shook—
beat and bleat and bled
swift divisions of earth.
Grabbed, then repossessed.

I could not keep up with it.

So they put me down
to become one with them—
hewer of wood, drawer of water,
too close to the ground with gross habits,

an unfeeling hearer
of the pure music.

VIII

We married beneath its cavity—
its mouth became our chapel
until a piece cracked
and it went dumb—our lives
of molten metal, of diamond, of emerald,
of plates of gold created
the calf we rode on

until struck down
by its weak hollow.
Fleas, serpents, gnats
made of the earth a crawling carpet.
Then silence followed the fits,
there was no need

for clock, no need for curfew
or matin. The unsound
clapper hung quiet.
Until everything started up again—
a bell converted into a cannon,
then reassembled into a bell.

We married beneath its cavity—
its mouth became our chapel . . .

IX

I slept in an induced coma
after the aneurysm—that heathen burst
upon the mind. I didn't know.

I was standing. Then fallen.

My family wept. When I awoke,
the talk was simple.
We laughed. We joked. We missed
death. No one paid

attention to the wars—The Word:
*The Nada Brahma. The Anahata Nadam.
The Saute Surmad.* The Original Tone
of the World. Itinerant sounds rang

from the stagnant waters, the mount
became the bottom of the sea
and the sea the arid land.
All was lurch and twist

and rupture in the volcanic globe head.
Only the bells—their sound so sad
on the wind—fled
to Rome for confession.

It's so real in the myth.

It was Passion Week. I watched
soap operas, sitcoms, reality TV—

women with low-slung jeans,
men with gelled hair.
All bodies waxed and oiled.

On Easter Sunday they polished my nails
and we traveled to the church
and to the returned,

cleansed, melancholy bells.

X

After the kingdom fell,
I pressed my head against the storm
window and watched
a cracked, quiet bell fallen
into the crotch of an olive tree.
All internal dialogue—
that self-hypnotic litany
of sound—consumed
my mind loop, a mantra burdened
by too many syllables, myself
a tower of babble. I couldn't follow
the rhythms of my voice.
After the kingdom fell

I saw others offer
a gold watch, a wedding band,
a silver spoon, a thimble,
wanting so much to melt
the present back into the past.
No one could break through the break-

proof glass. They couldn't hear
my heaved breath,
the point, pointed to—their hunched
faces, their downcast backs
turned away, they wouldn't see

the bell, the olive tree, the branch.

XI

I tie a string of bells around my ankle.
I am told I make a jingle
of delight. Sometimes, when I dance
I think my feet might burst.
Yet, I toll of my own accord.
I am not the maiden who threw herself

into the melting pot so that the metals
would fuse—perfect the sound—
make the air notes sweet and strong.
I am *not* that sacrifice.
Still, when my toes toss off
the earth, I can frighten away

the browsing snake.
I know someday I might break
and close my eyes to that scare,
pretend I glow like ruby and sapphire,
am a choir of tinkle and chime—
dainty, joyful, charmed, and wayward.

XII

I wore them with such pride—
the lead cow in the parade,
the fool in the Shakespeare play.
I was the hated mistress of the house,
with a tinkling sound braided
into my long hair, sewn into
the hems of my silk gowns.
It gave the servants notice
to be ready of my every need—

a tea cake, the tightening of my sash.
In my garden on the primavera tree,
haloed with gold
petals and laced with iron
chains, bells swung—
my favorite a rustic maiden
with puffed skirts,
her legs welded together
to form the clapper.

No one could ever enter her.

So many hollow cavities
with the day and night
ringing my head to banging.

horse bell cat bell dog bell ox bell
sleigh bell—a jingle in the silent snow—
ankle bell clap bell harness bell wind bell
muffin bell—a drool in the hunger mouth—
gate bell temple bell mass bell chant bell
donkey bell sheep bell sleep bell wake bell
More And More

my ornate rooms spun
spires higher, openings slant
enough where heavy missiles
could be dropped. The blood

music all ways running
in and out of the bells.

The Crosses

I

A sliver of the True Cross
lodged in the index finger
of my right hand. I thought

the "good" swastika lost—
its arms debossed
with symbols of the four winds:
top—an arrow—cold north
left—a star—sharp east
bottom—the sun—warm south
and a heart—gentle west.
Through the years it slowly spun
then, suddenly, flung out.
Killed millions. Arms fallen off.

A sliver of the True Cross
lodged in the index finger
of my right hand. I thought

of cutting off the branches
of the noble oak
except for two on opposite sides
to form a giant cross. The Cross
on which He died was made of oak—
about ten feet high,
like the one outside my door.

A sliver of the True Cross
lodged in the index finger
of my right hand. I thought

about the leaves in Eden
on the Tree of Life
(*I wanted to die*)
how they had the power to ease pain.
My finger swelled a red line
that traveled to my brain.

Pieces of the True Cross
could be healed from. I thought

I went and stood on
the Hill of the Skull
so near the Garden Tomb.
My room was dimly lit and hot
with a cloud of foul perfume.
Now, so near my heart, the splinter
stopped. As if blessed, *I thought*

for now, this must be
the gentle wind of the west.

(therapy i)

I am being taught the cross-
stitch on an even weave
fabric. I love my little
linen piece of territory,
its thread and pattern
with regulated boundaries.
It rests my mind from all intrusions—
the grab, snap, rip—
the unraveling—at borders.
No one wants my cloth—

my simple yellow flower.

II

On my way to the Holy Land
I passed effigies of knights
stretched out on their tombs,
their legs a display of precise twists
to exhibit how many crusades they fought.
On my way, I couldn't find

the promised dry path through the sea,
though I looked and looked.
Two boats sunk, but I was saved—

the good child who believes
what is told to me. On my way

I saw a man crucified on an X-
shaped cross, his immobile legs
on winged display. Another, hung
head down with feet stretched up—
the martyred, at once awkward
and lovely. I saw a man

in a loincloth, his side was pierced,
his legs were crossed.
I stared, then forced myself

to look away. *The good child who does*
what is taught to me—

to find the fragment of wood
within the gold and jeweled
reliquary—ruby for blood,
beryl for rebirth, pearl for purity.

The good child who tries to do
what is asked of me—
when I arrived, I dug through layers

of dirt to discover
the container disappeared, the land emptied.
I couldn't go home
with nothing to share.

The good child buries herself there.

(therapy ii)

I chose the trinket box—
4" x 6"—so as not to collect
too much, this first day
of the fall equinox—
the light on its fast fade—
and a circular design

to reflect time's twist and flow—
the complexity of life.
I like the loft of such a thought.
Think it a stitch
(the sick like to pun)

that will be its lid—
the half-shut eye of an idea.
I marvel at how tiny

the tools are that I've been given—
the blunt little
needle, the fragile threads—
yet am allowed the autumn colors—

so overheated.

III

Above the head a group of angels,
below a dove,
one side two Marys,
one the mother,
the other, the other
side two Johns, disciple
and Russian warrior,
at the foot an open tomb
with the always waiting skull.
Everywhere a canvas of reminders.
Cross of pearl, ivory, Whitby jet.
Hung from the neck, of wounds
of wood from a sunk ship,
of bones that seemed out of reach—
then a safe haven's sudden breach.

IV

Two Testaments to hang a man,
tree of mistletoe (*kiss kiss*)
to make a cross of knowledge (*slap slap*)
to be double-crossed, so hard to keep track
of the track (Cain always there to Abel's back)
on the back of the chair made of pine—
its lattice of crosses.

How I still pine for her

(*this sickness—the growth—pun*)
in her pine box,
the Star of David nailed to it
(six points, two triangles that intersect
at opposing angles, not the five
points for His wounds.)

I wear so many collars
of hope from cervical to cervix—

need a cane (*there I go, again*)
to lift me up, help me
forget the man who dupes—
his hug then stab.
My clogged mind a mélange
of hodge and podge—

those two old goats. Adam,

are you the blessed first man
or the Devil at the foot
of His Cross? I crisscross
the wood weave of my split chair

with my infected fingertips,
genuflect to the night star
whose points I cannot count
on, thrust a wish to it
with apish neck,

heavy with history
and its confounding amulets.

(therapy iii)

I am tired of stitching on
the Autumn Sampler.
I've been here before
with the discolored leaves.
Seven years I sew
the days together, tired
with her not being here.
Tired of wanting to go there.
Tired of the suggested
new materials—perforated paper,
silk, waste canvas—and new threads—
rayon, wool, metallic.
They'd only make my sampler gaudier.
Once, she gave me a cottage
made of single-ply pure cotton thread,
put it in a yellow frame.
It hung above my corner.
When I looked up, it seemed so simple.
I couldn't see the somersault,
the double running, the tied hem—
all the stitches and the knots it took
to create that little house.

V

Cross my fingers, cross my heart,
arms extended, legs together, not apart,
I make of myself a cross.
In my pockets bright blue beads,
small clay gods, scarabs,
four-leaf clovers, bejeweled mezuzahs.
In my hat cockleshells
to exorcize the demons,
to keep hidden the seventh chakra,
the tonsure, the bald compulsion.
Cross my fingers, cross my heart,
arms extended, legs together, not apart.
In my ears little bells of confusion
to frighten away eyes of evil.
On my breast a foul sachet
to repel the lick of the Devil.
Cross my fingers, cross my heart.
In my window a glass witch ball
to guard against the shatter
from intruders.
Cross my fingers.

(therapy iv)

Holly and Berries, Church in Winter,
Assisi Rose, Oxeye Daisy with Poppy Spray,
Birdhouse, Beehive, Black Cat,
Prancing Deer, Stained-Glass Angel, Celtic Cross,
even the Beaded Pansy Scissor Keeper—
made to tie to the handle of the small sharp edges—
make it easier to find—that gracefully
slide past each other, quick cut
all measures of thread, is of little consequence,
though its delicate stork head—
how it opens, shuts, births
the skin to lattice blood patterns—
is worthy of notice. I learn
to make of myself the canvas.

VI

At the crossroads outside of town,
past consecrated ground,
where the aimless move
their feet in the dust,
make an *X,* not anywhere
close to Jerusalem on that eminence
where the rocks are cleft,
beyond the Damascus Gate.
Find me far away near

the strip malls and motels
for daytime use
with no mourning adornment of cost—
no Whitby jet, no onyx, no gutta-percha,
just a ring encircled with plastic seed pearls
wreathed with one twisted strand of hair.

Soon, the nicked wardrobe will be emptied,
the drawers cleansed—
gone the magnifying
mirror, the tweezers, the sponge.

VII

The Lamb, The Laurel, The Lily, The Lion,
The Lamp, The Globe, The Palm, The Dove,
The Phoenix, The Pelican, The Staff, The Star,
The Gourd, The Shell, The Triangle, The Trefoil.

Everywhere the symbols. On the ceiling.
On the wall. Under the skin—
The waiting skull. In the mirror

The Peacock—all vainglory. Always,
The Serpent—coil of sin, sphere of wisdom.
Three Fishes interlaced in the pitch
night aquarium. *Baptism*

of everyone . . . Baptism of no one . . .

(therapy v)

I am the cross
stitching my initials
into the pincushion,
the doll's house rug,
the baby's bib,
leaving my mark against
the blank space
just like she did
when she left the alphabet
of the sunflower,
of the ark—its animal glory—
of the heart
on the christening gown.
I am the cross
stitching the poems
on antique white linen.
The doctors are quite pleased.
For the moment
I am calm.

Widdershins

I

Turn counter to the clock
tick, its annoying tic,
stir the pot
left to right, set
the table west to east,
steer the small boat
from the harbor
against the sun path.

Traveling the heavens
has not led to protection.

II

Sleep naked in moonlight under
the Full Wolf Moon, Full
Hunger Moon, Full Worm
Moon, Full Egg Moon, Full
Milk Moon, Full
Red Moon, Full Hunter's
Moon, Full Beaver
Moon, Full Buck
Moon, sleep struck

swallowed in its sense—
the lunacy of its light.

III

Once, I touched wood,
made the sign of the cross,
tossed salt over my left shoulder,
used spit on cards and letters,
on my right shoe before the journey,
on the wind to stop the storm.
All tug and twist and traipse
for luck magic. I did.

Now, I curl into the owl's nest,
make it my house, sleep
with that nocturnal bird of unrest,
its melancholy breast pressed
into my heart,
see sunlight only
when I haul out my rubbish.

Await the curse.

IV

Only a backward spin

my mangled body threaded
through spokes of the leaden wheel,
seated in the spiked metal
interrogation chair—the agony
from beneath. The crown of my head
shoved into the steel cap, the huge screw
tightened at the top, my pressured skull
drilling my teeth into my jaw, eyes out.
The tongue of confession,

then forgiveness, nowhere to be heard—
screaming, I am

running through the blade
grass. Away from the sun,
his unleashed, slash, god advance,
his rage all ways
disassembling me—

this time, to plant. Now, made
to look up, forever face his gaze

if I am to survive.

V

I plucked the Devil's Guts—
Strangle Tare, Witch's Hair—
the dodder. Used the wiry, gnarled
lace as cord for knot magic.
My mind alive in a warty place.

Mother tried to make me stop,

told me to drink water from a stump
or blood from the eel for a cure.
We encircled the coarse
lesions with silk thread,
rubbed them with two halves of an apple.

It was not a time of reason.

She tied a love sachet—pink cloth—
3 parts Lavender, 2 parts Rose Petal,
1 part Orrisroot, around my waist.

She cried: *Be patient for a proper love.*

I thought: *Wait Why Waste.*
And dug deeper into the night
ground, found him again,
his throat all puffed and ready
to make his flutelike sound.
His skin was rough—vivid

with red spots—his tongue
was sticky, quick, and long.

VI

Ointment rubbed over the skin—
3 drops Frankincense,
2 drops Peppermint,
1 drop Clove, 1 drop Pine—
could not bring on the exorcism.
All hands blunt clumsy.
Too much food had been eaten.
Egg and chop and leg of duck

were placed on the breast
of the dead one,
then passed to my lone figure
in the corner—*the sin eater*
of the family *chewing, chewing*
so the beloved's soul could be free,
made light to have
an easy journey.

VII

I sit forever and stare
at the scar disappear,
that will not. The Purple-
Bellied Foxglove does not
calm my heart. Love
Apples of the Mandrake
turn rot soft in my palm.
Angelica with its chaste white
flower refuses my unholy hand.
Even the Opium Poppy does not
lead me to the promised land of deep,
forgetful sleep. Only the inky

juice of Nightshade
gives me a pause of escape—
distorts my sight—
as does the lace-topped stalks
of Hemlock—its nectar spread
on my skin where it is most thin.
I fly from my chair

where I sit forever and stare
at the scar disappear,
that will not, then return
to my room, that depression—
the ravaged land of the wound.

VIII

Always there, the innuendo, implication,
then the incineration in the witch oven—
the fire-scorched belly of the bronze bull,
the eyelet curtain–laced crematorium.

Thumbscrews, leg vises for the early stages
to force an admission, the strappado
waiting in the corner along with the mercy
of the sword. The bearing

of all torture just makes the inquisitor
angrier. The *Malleus*—the "how-to" book—
held tight, is bound in human skin,
as is the handle of the bayonet,

the shade of this lamp,
that gives off such a light.

IX

The iron shame
mask fit tight over the slack
muscles in my face.
It had elongated ears for how
I strained to overhear,
a stretched nose for how
I poked around to know,
a snake tongue for how
my talk at times held venom.
The inner spikes
of its mouthpiece sliced
the insides of my cheeks.
Dazed, I wandered the town
against the stare of the sun,
saw the ridicule in
others' eyes as they saw
the same in mine.
Not much difference
in our glance,
nor our lives—
just the luck of bad chance.

X

Mugwort, Sweet Pea, Thistle,
Arbutus, Sandalwood, Mallow,
Bloodroot, Fig, Yarrow,
Cattail, Lily, Lotus,
Anise, Cowslip, Myrtle,
Apple, Amaranth, Fennel,
Yew. *You* under the green grass
under the willow, tell me,

what do I string, brew,
bury, drink—what
should I honor, burn

for the answers?

XI

Pay the torturer by the ounce in pure silver—receptive
as the bloated moon so full of itself
to convince, overwhelm—to carry you down
the unending corridor:

Thrashing and whipping (add rope and/or rods).

Crushing thumb or other limbs, then resetting (salve extra).

*Strangling, then burning (again, the rope, plus
the igniting of the stake).*

*Beheading, then burning (same as above, plus
the use of a sword).*

Breaking alive on the wheel (add chains).

*Cutting off a hand (again, the sword, plus
the necessary cloth).*

Cutting out the tongue (small knife, tongs).

The night traveler knows voice comes with a price,
as does its sunk shadow—silence.

XII

Eventually the scars become glitter
on the skin—small stars. The damage
caused by what or who, a journey
into a hidden solar system—night-
mares (spectral horses galloping
through a galaxy of terror). My bed
is placed toward the door under
a crossbeam in the ceiling, crosswise
over the floorboards, in the direction corpses
are carried out—feet first.
The rays of the moon fall across
its sheets—always messed.
Each morning they invite all
spirits to come in and rest.

I would like to sleep now—dream less,

but someone has hung a blackbird's
right wing on the closet hook
and no matter how I try not
to look at it—I look.

Afterwor(l)d

KNOWLEDGE

Where the Tigris and Euphrates meet
is the Tree cemented in concrete.
The fruit all picked and eaten,
the bald branches broken.
Where the Tigris and the Euphrates meet
the holy road, once filled with date palms
and wild geraniums wandering every bush,
is smothered with bombed-out bridges
and scorched tanks and peddlers
with their fractured stands
that hold the spoiled apple and orange.
Where the Tigris and the Euphrates meet
the dried mother womb sleeps,
buried under slabs of tongues and rubble talk—
the wetland drained, the marsh a small weep,
the garden above starved for its life.
Where the Tigris and the Euphrates meet
all that's left is the knowledge warned of.

MONKSHOOD

I wait next to Cerberus,
watch his mouth froth
rise up to the earth.
The hunters are baiting the wolves,
the armies poisoning the wells
with it, while I wait
at the gates of Hades

for Romeo to swallow it—
descend and save the one
he's not yet met,
the one whom he cannot live

without.
Sick romantic, in death
I am always lovely.
So I wait for him

to join me. Bind me
to his passion story.
It is and forever was my great wish
for I have waited All Time
next to Cerberus.

13

13 years I lived in a house with the number 13

—

the total for a witches' coven, the tarot card reserved
for death, the people present at the Supper
where Judas was the final guest

—

I've betrayed at least myself 13 times,
though I'd rather not remember

—

in my house there were 13 stairs to step
to my writing nook

—

I never got closer to God however high I looked

—

the crossroads of town are 13 blocks from here to there—
no matter where you are

—

the suicides are buried there, so their spirits will get confused,
not know which way to go when they try to get back home

—

a bell rang 13 times when I died, but it had no rope or ringer,
a bad omen most agreed

—

although the Egyptians believed 13

-

the last rung on the ladder

-

that the soul had to seize to begin

-

its flow into eternity

CLEAN

Still, against the heavy wind,
the spoon of cherrywood

no longer moves
the liquid in the pot.

Locked in the lamplight sweat
of the eternal night winter,

the disturbed quiet is quite safe—
suffocates the closed room.

Looking out, all that can be
seen is a knothole in the oak tree.

Gone is the fig, the oyster, the mango,
the red candle—its wick.

Gone is the bean, the blackberry, the carrot,
the parsnip, the horn of the rhinoceros.

The cupboard is both
emptied and latched.

The man in his blister heat
will not come back.

The kitchen is so clean,
everything's in its nook.

Susan Hahn is a poet, a playwright, and the editor of *TriQuarterly* magazine. She is the author of eight books of poetry and the recipient of numerous awards for her poems, including a Guggenheim Fellowship in 2003. The *Chicago Tribune* named her fourth book, *Holiday,* and her fifth book, *Mother in Summer,* among the best books of 2002. Her first play, *Golf,* premiered in 2005, and *The Scarlet Ibis,* her previous book of poetry, was performed as a verse play in 2007 and will be reprised in 2008.